Further praise for

Magdalene

"A poignant portrait of contemporary womanhood. . . . This newest collection aptly demonstrates the particular strengths of Howe's wry, bittersweet talent."
—*Library Journal*, starred review

"Each book of Marie Howe's is a singular accomplishment, but none is as wildly alive as this. How does she see with such devastating clarity? Or allow so much of 'what the living do' onto the page: avoidance, longing, tenderness, resentment, and desire? What makes the engine go? The wry, knowing, seeking voice of Mary Magdalene, worn like the most transparent of masks. The experience of mothering a daughter, a long arc of love building its house in the years. Howe sweeps up a life and fixes it on the page, and stands here before us, the stunned and grateful witness of all that's taken and granted by love and time."   —Mark Doty

"Marie Howe is among our most gifted poets of trauma and healing, and of where the everyday encounters the world of the sacred. In *Magdalene*, Howe raises the ante. She now channels the 'woman taken in adultery' of New Testament legend, and she is also her questing self, lover and mother, risen to the exaltation of the possible."   —Alicia Ostriker, author of *The Book of Seventy*

"Gorgeous, ferocious, lacerating, sexy, and profoundly compassionate. I could swear the book emitted light when I put it down on my bedside table and turned off the lamp."
                                                                        —Michael Cunningham

"Marie Howe has always come as close as any poet since Rilke to touching eternity, simply by stretching out her hand and believing that something exists beyond her grasp, beyond her knowing. Here, with *Magdalene*, she somehow goes even deeper, into what it is to both be alive and a manifestation of the divine. I am, once again, in awe of her powers, at their fullest here."
                                                                        —Nick Flynn

Magdalene

poems

MARIE HOWE

W. W. Norton & Company

Independent Publishers Since 1923

New York | London

For information about permission to reproduce selections from this book,
write to Permissions, W. W. Norton & Company, Inc.,
500 Fifth Avenue, New York, NY 10110

For information about special discounts for bulk purchases, please contact
W. W. Norton Special Sales at specialsales@wwnorton.com or 800-233-4830

Manufacturing by LSC Communications, Harrisonburg
Book design by Chris Welch
Production manager: Lauren Abbate

Library of Congress Cataloging-in-Publication Data

Names: Howe, Marie, 1950– author.
Title: Magdalene : poems / Marie Howe.
Description: First edition. | New York : W. W. Norton & Company, [2017]
Identifiers: LCCN 2016046271 | ISBN 9780393285307 (hardcover)
Classification: LCC PS3558.O8925 A6 2017 | DDC 811/.54—dc23
LC record available at https://lccn.loc.gov/2016046271

ISBN 978-0-393-35603-8 pbk.

W. W. Norton & Company, Inc.
500 Fifth Avenue, New York, N.Y. 10110
www.wwnorton.com

W. W. Norton & Company Ltd.
15 Carlisle Street, London W1D 3BS

2 3 4 5 6 7 8 9 0

CONTENTS

ACKNOWLEDGMENTS

I wish to thank the following magazines where some of these poems first appeared:

The New Yorker: "Fourteen"; "Low Tide, Late August"

Provincetown Arts: "On Men, Their Bodies"; "Magdalene at the Theopoetics Conference"; "Before the Beginning"; "If this line is the beginning"

Ploughshares: "Waiting at the River"

The American Poetry Review: "Magdalene—The Seven Devils"; "How the Story Started"; "The Affliction"; "What I Did Wrong"; "Magdalene: Her Dream of Integration"; "Magdalene and the Interior Life"; "Magdalene: The Addict"; "The Disciples"; "Magdalene Afterwards"; "The Adoption: When the Girl Arrived"; "The Girl at 3"

So many friends have given close attention to the poems in this collection, and inspiration in their own lives and work—too many to list here. But there would be no *Magdalene* without Lucille Clifton, Mark Conway, Mark Doty, Eve Ensler, Nick Flynn, Brenda Hillman, Grace Inan Howe, Michael Klein, Mary LaChapelle, Donna Masini, Richard McCann, Jim Moore, Martin Moran, Elaine Pagels, Spencer Reece, Victoria Redel, Tom Sleigh and Lili Taylor.

Thank you to William White and the Crowley/Friedman family.

Thank you to my editor Jill Bialosky for her insight and care.

To Bill Clegg for his steady encouragement.

Thank you to Bill and Sonya Dunham, true village people, grand and generous spirits, who gave us the miracle of the extra room.

Thank you Grace Inan Howe for the cover photograph.

His disciples said, When will you be visible to us?
and when will we see you?
He said, When you undress and are not ashamed.

—*The Gospel According to Thomas*

Before the Beginning

Was I ever virgin?

Did someone touch me before I could speak?

Who had me before I knew I was an I?

So that I wanted that touch again and again

without knowing who or why or from whence it came?

Magdalene—The Seven Devils

Mary, called Magdalene, from whom seven devils had been cast out —*Luke 8:2*

The first was that I was very busy.

The second—I was different from you: whatever happened to you could

not happen to me, not like that.

The third—I worried.

The fourth—envy, disguised as compassion.

The fifth was that I refused to consider the quality of life of the aphid,

The aphid disgusted me. But I couldn't stop thinking about it.

The mosquito too—its face.   And the ant—its bifurcated body.

Ok   the first was that I was so busy.

The second that I might make the wrong choice,

because I had decided to take that plane that day,

that flight, before noon, so as to arrive early

and, I shouldn't have wanted that.

The third was that if I walked past the certain place on the street

the house would blow up.

The fourth was that I was made of guts and blood with a thin layer

of skin lightly thrown over the whole thing.

The fifth was that the dead seemed more alive to me than the living.

The sixth—if I touched my right arm I had to touch my left arm, and if I touched the left arm a little harder than I'd first touched the right then I had

to retouch the left and then touch the right again so it would be even.

The seventh—I knew I was breathing the expelled breath of everything that

was alive, and I couldn't stand it.

I wanted a sieve, a mask, a—I hate this word—a cheesecloth—

to breathe through that would trap it—whatever was inside everyone else that

entered me when I breathed in.

No. That was the first one.

The second was that I was so busy. I had no time. How had this happened?

How had our lives gotten like this?

The third was that I couldn't eat food if I really saw it—distinct, separate

from me in a bowl or on a plate.

Ok. The first was that. I could never get to the end of the list.

The second was that the laundry was never finally done.

The third was that no one knew me, although they thought they did.

And that if people thought of me as little as I thought of them then

what was love?

The fourth was I didn't belong to anyone. I wouldn't allow myself to belong

to anyone.

The fifth was that I knew none of us could ever know what we didn't know.

The sixth was that I projected onto others what I myself was feeling.

The seventh was the way my mother looked when she was dying,

the sound she made—her mouth wrenched to the right and cupped open

so as to take in as much air . . . the gurgling sound, so loud

we had to speak louder to hear each other over it.

And that I couldn't stop hearing it—

years later—grocery shopping, crossing the street—

No, not the sound—it was her body's hunger

finally evident—what our mother had hidden all her life.

For months I dreamt of knucklebones and roots,

the slabs of sidewalk pushed up like crooked teeth by what grew underneath.

The underneath. That was the first devil. It was always with me.

And that I didn't think you—if I told you—would understand any of this—

Looking down at him my tears fell onto his chest

and he looked back at me with such pity

raising his hand to wipe my cheek

before he wrapped his arms around me and pulled me

down to the bed so he could press inside me deeper

On Men, Their Bodies

One penis was very large and thick so when he put it inside me I really did say, Wow. One penis was uncircumcised, and I loved to grip the shaft and pull down so the head popped out like a little man. One penis was curved so I had to move in a different way. One penis was so friendly I was never afraid of it. One penis was so slender I was startled. One penis was blunt and short like a little pig. One penis couldn't harden until he stuffed it soft inside me. One penis came as soon as I started to move. I'm so sorry, he said I have a problem, but I didn't care. I loved that boy. One penis pressed against me hard almost every morning, but I got out of bed as if I hadn't heard a word it had said. One penis was so dear to me I kissed it and kissed it even after I knew it had been with someone else. One penis I never saw, but my hand came to know it from the outside of his jeans. One penis loved the inside of my mouth so much it sang, it sputtered. One had a name. One was a mouse. One, he

explained to me, had very very tiny crabs, so we couldn't have sex for a while.

One was Orthodox and wouldn't touch blood. One had a mole, a hard little

dot just under the rim. One penis was extremely patient without making a big

deal about it. One penis had a great sense of humor. One penis had herpes

but I didn't know that word yet. One was a battering ram. One was a drunk

staggering, a lout, a bully. One slept inside me, comfortably at home.

How the Story Started

I was driven toward desire by desire.

believing that the fulfillment of that desire was an end.

There was no end.

Others might have looked into the future and seen

a shape inside the coming years—

a house, a child, a man who might be a help.

I saw his back bent over what he was working on,

the back of his neck, how he stood in his sneakers,

and wanted to eat him.

How could I see another person, I mean who *he* was—apart from me—

apart from that?

Thorns

I pressed them through my hair into my head

pressed them into my waistband and

later into my palms,

a secret intimacy among those thorns and me

a love

(from whom or to whom it mattered less than

that it was) and that

it was

was the evidence of love:

and so a comfort in the small

pain they brought.

The Affliction

When I walked across a room I saw myself walking

as if I were someone else,

when I picked up a fork, when I pulled off a dress,

as if I were in a movie.

It's what I thought you saw when you looked at me.

So when I looked at you, I didn't see you

I saw the me I thought you saw, as if I were someone else.

I called that *outside*—watching. Well I didn't call it anything

when it happened all the time.

But one morning after I stopped the pills—standing in the kitchen

for one second I was *inside* looking out.

Then I popped back outside. And saw myself looking.

Would it happen again? It did, a few days later.

My friend Wendy was pulling on her winter coat, standing by the kitchen door

and suddenly I was *inside* and I saw her.

I looked out from my own eyes

and I saw: her eyes: blue gray   transparent

and inside them: Wendy herself!

Then I was outside again,

and Wendy was saying, Bye-bye, see you soon,

as if Nothing Had Happened.

She hadn't noticed. She hadn't known that I'd Been There

for Maybe 40 Seconds,

and that then I was Gone.

She hadn't noticed that I Hadn't Been There for Months,

years, the entire time she'd known me.

I needn't have been embarrassed to have been there for those seconds;

she had not Noticed The Difference.

This happened on and off for weeks,

and then I was looking at my old friend John:

: suddenly I was in: and I saw him,

and he: (and this was almost unbearable)

he saw me see him,

and I saw him see me.

He said something like, You're going to be ok now,

or, It's been difficult hasn't it,

but what he said mattered only a little.

We met—in our mutual gaze—in between

a third place I'd not yet been.

The Split

Then a voice inside my head

began to speak, and it said, *You are doing this now,*

Now you're doing that: company I couldn't speak of.

What would the voice say if I spoke?

My father, swaying in the doorway, said, I'll break you.

Who would I be if I broke?

No you won't, I said,

and the voice cleared its throat.

What I Did Wrong

Slapped the man's face, then slapped it again,

broke the plate, broke the glass, pushed the cat

from the couch with my feet. Let the baby

cry too long, then shook him,

let the man walk, let the girl down,

wouldn't talk, then talked too long,

lied when there was no need

and stole what others had, and never

told the secret that kept me apart from them.

Years holding on to a rope

that wasn't there, always sorry

righteous and wrong. Who would

follow that young woman down the narrow hallway?

Who would call her name until she turns?

His cheek against my cheek,

his mouth on my mouth, his hands on my hair

to be gathered close   closer

This was the source of my suffering and joy

Magdalene on Romance

I wanted him to stop drinking, to make

the bed, to pay attention, to wear shoes

instead of sneakers. I'd explain him to

himself so well he would come to love

as someone comes to a good idea.

I was a door slammer and a screamer

a professor, an explainer—a dog

instructing ducks.

Unlucky in love, I said, as one, then another

turned and walked, or I turned and left.

The screen door banged a few times, then stopped.

How quiet the room then,

when I sat down in the white wooden chair.

Magdalene: The Addict

I liked Hell,

I liked to go there alone

relieved to lie in the wreckage, ruined, physically undone.

The worst had happened. What else could hurt me then?

I thought it was the worst, thought nothing worse could come.

Then nothing did, and no one.

Magdalene and the Interior Life

The pills were an army of white knights

and yellow and blue and green

and yellow and red.

The pills were the floorboards

and the bright lights that made what's what possible.

They kept everything down—no laughter,

no out-of-control laughing or terror

no pictures either—which is what I hadn't noticed

all those years until I stopped.

Was it weeks later? months?

Suddenly an apple (I saw it!!

An image of an apple inside my self!)

What?

Then a tree.

An elephant (inside my head!),

A wagon pulled by horses, a wooden wagon

the wheels squeaking along the rutted road.

—the smell of dirt and water!

The tinny plop sound of falling rain filling

 a tin can left out on a stone porch . . .

I imagined it!

Can you understand? I didn't know until they came back

that the images had gone away for so long.

Like shy or frightened animals, slowly they came back.

The Landing

I stood beside the high cupboard that covered

the radiator in the hall (inside the drawers: the odd pencils and pins

we couldn't find when we needed them)

near the front stairs that rose up and turned by the high windows.

What did we call that space? The landing.

All the pills had brought me to that place

And I understood that if I kept it all up . . .

no one would know me.

A dim light far in the distance? No.

To love—I had to be there.

I had to be there to be loved.

Magdalene: The Woman Taken in Adultery

Teacher, they said to Jesus, The law of Moses says to stone her. What do you say? —*John 8:5*

You know how it is when your speeding car spins on the ice at night

and you think *here it is?*

When the deer spring across the headlights?

When you begin to slip down the steep and icy steps?

Now imagine someone is about to push you, someone you know

and then they don't.

Magdalene: The Next Day

The world that would have gone on without me

bargained and clattered

and I walked where I wanted, free of the pretense of family now,

belonging to no one

back to the place where he'd bent and written in the dust.

(He was man among men—he knew not to look at them)

Whatever he'd scribbled in the dust wasn't there anymore,

but he was

standing with his friends in the shade of the temple wall.

The Teacher

When Moses pleaded, and Yaweh agreed at last to let the people

hear His voice,

it's said that he allowed each person to hear what each could bear

to the very brim of that and no more.

Afterwards the people said, Please Moses, from now on you listen.

We don't want to hear it. You do the talking and listening now.

Being with the teacher was a little like that

as though he were a book too difficult to read.

So, I thought I had to become more than I was, more than I'd been.

but that wasn't it. It seemed rather that

something had to go. Something had to be let go of.

It wasn't that I saw something new—or saw suddenly into him,

not that, not ever

but that the room itself, whatever room we might be standing in,

assumed an astonishing clarity:

and the things in the room: a table, a cup, a meowing cat.

The Disciples

I suppose it's always like that with a teacher.

Everyone wanted his gaze as if it were water at noon.

But it was women who made the food,

women who opened their homes to us,

their quiet daughters standing in the doorway,

the little ones being told to let him rest, let him eat,

and they hadn't cooked a dish.

It was still the old way

although they all talked about the new way, the new way.

For me it was different.

I knew that even when he seemed not to be looking at me, he was.

But of course I was wrong about that too.

Magdalene on Gethsemane

When he went to the garden the night before

And fell with his face to the ground

what he imagined was not his torture, not his own death

     That's what the story says, but that's not what he told me.

He said he saw the others   *the countless*   in his name

raped, burned, lynched, stoned, bombed, beheaded, shot, gassed,

gutted and raped again.

Calvary

Someone hanging clothes on a line between buildings,

someone shaking out a rug from an open window

might have heard hammering, one or two blocks away

and thought little or nothing of it.

Magdalene Afterwards

Remember the woman in the blue burka forced to kneel in the stadium

then shot in the head?   That was me.

And I was the woman who secretly filmed it.

I was hung as a witch by the people in my own town

I was sent to the asylum at sixteen.

I was walking with my younger sister looking for firewood

when we saw the group of men approaching.

I'm the woman so in love with my husband

sometimes I wait in the kitchen chair and stare at the door.

I'm bored at the business meeting,

impatient with the Do Not Walk sign.

I'm parked in my wheelchair with the others in the hallway

in the home—three hours till lunch, I don't remember who it is

who leans down to kiss me.

I've forgotten my keys, dropped the dish, fallen down

the icy stoop.

I'm sitting on the bench with my bags, waiting for the bus.

I'm the woman in the black suit and heels hailing a taxi.

I'm in prayer, in meditation, I've shaved my head, I wear robes

now instead of dresses.

When I enter the classroom, all the children call out my name at once.

I'm talking on my cell phone while driving.

I'm walking the goats out to the far field, gazing at the mountain

I've looked at every day of my life.

I never had children,

I bore nine living children and two dead ones

I adopted a girl in my late middle age

I'm cooking rice and beans

cooking dal

cooking lamb

reheating pizza

lighting the candles on the birthday cake

standing quietly by the window

still hungry for I don't know what.

Often I'm lonely.

Sometimes a joy pours through me so immense.

I want to see through the red bricks of the building across the street,

into the something else that almost gleams through the day.

Low Tide, Late August

That last summer when everything was almost always terrible

we waded into the bay one late afternoon as the tide had almost finished

pulling all the way out

and sat down in the waist-deep water

I floating on his lap facing him, my legs floating around him,

and we quietly coupled,

and stayed, loosely joined like that, not moving,

but being moved by the softly sucking and lapping water,

as the pulling out reached its limit and the tide began to flow slowly back again.

Some children ran after each other, squealing in the shallows, near but not too near.

I rested my chin on his shoulder looking toward the shore.

As he must have been looking over my shoulder, to where the water deepened

and the small boats tugged on their anchors.

How many times did he say it

Change doesn't hurt he'd say,

as much as the resistance to change

The Adoption: When the Girl Arrived

She took me from the place in the center where it was quiet,

where time falls as sunlight through a gauze curtain

and the animal in me slept and dreamed and stirred

(—a sleeping animal, running)

She pulled me from desire for a shoulder or a back

                                        a body pressed to my body

She pulled me from prayer and desire
                        from even the memory

the smell and sound of him moaning against me

the dark warm cave of want filled and filled and filled—stuffed

overstuffed.   That stopped.

The Girl at 3

The girl is in love with the letter M.

M, she says quietly to herself—smiling at the thought of it.

M, she says, out loud.

(The book I'm reading says that what we have to do,

within ourselves, to learn to read—creates a self,

but when we've created that self we've created an edge

that separates us from the world we long for

: the interiority we create by reading is rich and lonely.)

In the paintings of the Annunciation

Mary has looked up from her book to listen to the angel.

In some her finger keeps her place, as if she would

return to where she was, or to who she was after listening

(But she will not return)

Where is that angel? In the room?

Within the room her reading has made within her?

It's a European invention—the book, the girl, the curtained bed.

Mary couldn't read, and so—according to the book I'm reading

—didn't have a self,

not as we know it.

She held these things in her heart.

M! the girl says when she sees the letter on her letter board,

although it is in fact an N.

M! she shouts, in the way she shouts Home!

when we arrive there.

Magdalene on Surrender

Look a blue flower, the girl says this morning, bending down.

Look Mom, how high the tree is, as she looks up.

Then she runs away laughing, and won't get in the car.

This is my chair he would say—*get up.*

    This is my hair, he'd say, *I can touch it.*

I'll break you, he'd say.

Years after he was dead, when I finally said, You won,

the air took on a living color,

the pattern of the rug emerged, distinct, under my feet,

the tree I passed on Linnaean Street became a tree,

its bark unmoving.

No, not a tree   a telephone pole made from a tree.

That's what I put my hand on.

She wouldn't get in, running around the still-wet grass, laughing.

Then she did.

From the front seat I could hear her eating her banana

her soft mushy chewing, the scent brightening the messy car.

It didn't occur to me until much later

that when any of those men entered my body

he might have been trying to touch something

other than himself.

The Anima Alone

I'm sorry the girl says when she drops the berries on the kitchen floor.

I'm sorry she says when she spills the milk,

and looks too closely at her mother's face.

Don't keep saying you're sorry she says to the girl.

I'm sorry the girl says, I'll try not to say it again.

The News

The girls in their booster seats behind me are playing mermaids.

Hey mother mermaid! they call out

I'm listening to the car radio and the senator breaking down on the senate floor,

speaking against his party's nomination to the United Nations,

and I say Yes my mermaids, what is it? as the senator says, My colleagues tell me

Don't worry, but I think of my children, and my grandchildren

(And here he actually begins sobbing)

We're dead! The girls shout from the back

You're what? I say, Dead! they call out laughing. Be sad.

Boo hoo, I say, They're dead, I'm sad (still listening to the senator)

and then a sighing sort of singing comes from the back seat,

Wooooooooooo, we're spirits, the girls sing

—high and sweet as the lost song of a lost race—

and then—Now we're back!   Laughing, and dying

and coming back maybe a half dozen more times

before I pull into their preschool driveway and stop.

This chamber, the senator says, is ominously quiet.

Then one of the girls says, Now let's just one of us be dead.

And the other says, Ok.

And first girl says, Who? And the other says, You.

and the rest is history.

Christmas Eve

When I brought the girl to bed

    earlier that evening when the guests were still there

I'd noticed that the little manger we'd set up on the side table was empty—

    green light from the small bulb shining into empty space.

Later when I went to check on her, I saw she'd built a labyrinth of blocks,

    a very high tower in the center of the labyrinth

and on the top of this tower—an angel on its back,

    and at the foot of the tower—the clay baby Jesus and a lamb.

Where was Mary, and Joseph?

Here, she pointed out from her bed—wandering through the seemingly

endless corridors of the labyrinth—looking for their lost child.

Listening

From the front seat of the Honda

    when I sometimes turned the radio off,

from under the reading lamp, once or twice I did look up.

While riding the stationary bike, within what I rented

and renovated I did hear . . .

(I had to pick up the girl and stop at the store)

but every once in a while

        pulling the hangers along the rack,

rising up on the escalators of NIKETOWN with its piped-in sound of sweat and effort

or standing in the elevator alone.   Was it a shout?

I slumped in the chair watching *The Sopranos.*

                         An ocean far off?   Children screaming?

      I lay on the couch watching *Six Feet Under.*

Tell me—

Perhaps a person is being held for questioning.

And no one knows where that person is

or what will be done to her, and no one will ever know.

Does it matter—do you think—how that person conducts herself?

Waiting at the River

Sometimes, I'm tired of being a mother, weary of holding her in my mind, her words

brighter than mine, the light's movement on the rock. Look, I say, Listen, to what

my daughter said. (Tired of being) Reasonable and calm, answering to Mom,

and how sweet (the sound) my name in her mouth, her mouth on my name, her

mouth is not my mouth, her mind (not my). Her body has too many bites on it

(too many) scratched. I'm the post she touches and leaves, and (before she) leaves

(I'm) the base she runs to, and pushes off from: transparent home, ignored, rebuilt,

undone, restored (all) without her knowing, waiting to catch the shine off her hair

as she rounds the (watery) bend in the river, stepping among the stones. I stand up

(waving), stretch and stand up, to show her where I am.

The Teacher

Was he my husband, my lover, my teacher?

One book will say one thing. Another book another.

Can the body love beyond hunger?

You tell me what you know of desire and surrender.

I had a teacher who would not hurt me. I had a teacher

who struck me in the face, then struck me again.

I had a teacher who died in his own bed, a teacher who

died in public, a teacher who was a child, a girl.

Can we love without greed? Without wanting to be first?

Everyone wanted to pour his wine, to sit near him at the table.

Me too. Until he was dead.

Then he was with me all the time.

Conversation: Dualism

Is that bad? the girl says, when someone tells a story, or when we see

an accident on the road, or lately when almost anything happens.

Well, I say, not good, nor bad.

But is it bad? she says again, sensing my small

hesitation. Well,

not good, I say

—and that seals it.

Walking Home

Everything dies, I said. How had that started?

A tree? The winter? Not me, she said.

And I said, Oh yeah? And she said, I'm reincarnating.

Ha, she said, See you in a few thousand years!

Why years, I wondered, why not minutes? Days?

She found that so funny—Ha Ha—doubled over—

Years, she said, confidently.

I think you and I have known each other a few lifetimes, I said.

She said, I have never before been a soul on this earth.

(It was cold. We were hungry.) Next time, you be the mother, I said.

No way, Jose, she said, as we turned the last windy corner.

Magdalene: Her Dream of Integration

I wanted to make love with them both at the same time:

to place my hand there where his body extended into her body

to where her body received his body

—to feel the shaft of him

entering her and pulling out and pushing in—that

excited me almost unbearably—but I couldn't get to them,

wandering through the hotel halls, up this corridor, down that corridor,

mute with desire, I woke trembling.

I'm trembling now.

Fourteen

She is still mine—for another year or so,

but she's already looking past me

through the funeral-home door

to where the boys have gathered in their dark suits.

After the Funeral

Driving the thruway past the houses of the dead

and two miles west of that exit, the sky plumped with rain,

the girl and I listened to a downloaded book

tell us about another time, more gone than this one.

Does everything seen from a distance look pretty?

The deadly lightening, the southern town

where in 100 or so more pages a man will hang from a tree?

No man yet. The tree unmarked

I don't want to hear anymore, the girl said,

Something bad is going to happen.

Nearing home the sky turned biblical, pink and bruised purple,

half a rainbow pushing up like a plow handle broken off

while in the west more dark rain gathered so dense it seemed

anvil enough to hurt the car should we drive into it.

We drove into it, then out the other side

and finally up our own gravelly road and into the yard.

The dog bounded to the door.

We carried the bags from the car.

Adaptation

Last night, cleaning the counters after dinner, the girl said,

Would you want to know the date of your death?

No, I said, I would not want to know that.

I would she said.

Then she said, If someone killed you

would you want to come back for revenge?

No, I said, I'd rather come back to the people I loved.

What if you came back to someone and they'd forgotten you? she said

I'd tell them I loved them anyway, I said,

What if they said *Who?*

I scrubbed the pans for a while.

That night we decided to watch something other than the murder mysteries

we'd been watching for months

and chose an Edith Wharton adaptation,

wealthy young American girls flocking to England to acquire husbands

—every single one of them chose the wrong man.

Why do they all do that? I said from the couch;

and from the pink chair she said, Mom there wouldn't be any story

if they all chose well.

By the time the first episode was over we were in darkness,

both of us, wrapped in blankets shouting No no no no

when the last most vibrant girl agreed to marry the rich sop.

The credits rolled. 17 seconds to the next episode 16, 15, 14,

Another one? she said.

Sure, I said, looking at the clock.   And she clicked.

You know how it is

something has to put a stick in the spoke

to stop the wheel from spinning

and it occurs to you

what you thought was true is not at all, nope

and you glimpse the scrim through which

you've been gazing . . .

The Map

The failure of love might count for most of the suffering in the world.

The girl was going over her global studies homework in the air

where she drew the map with her finger

              touching the Goby Desert,

the Plateau of Tiber in front of her,

and looking through her transparent map backwards

I did suddenly see,

how her left is my right, and for a moment I understood.

The Visit

I could hardly look into his eyes,

    I looked more often at his mouth,

and could raise my eyes only briefly.

Watching my girl staring into his face

    debating with him, as I used to,

proud of herself, reveling in her beauty and will.

Your eyes are so blue, she said, and stared and stared.

Indeed they were as blue as when I first saw him so many years ago.

Shame might have kept me from raising my eyes to his.

All those arguments

All that kissing

Driving the car along that country road

with his hand inside me.

I couldn't look.

But after he left, when the girl was in bed

I lay awake a long time, gazing into the life I'd chosen.

Two Animals

This morning walking naked through the narrow hall

startling the girl who was climbing down the ladder from her loft—

she crouched, her eyes wide.

I seemed to see us both like that—the naked walking woman,

the crouching girl—two animals in the world.

You scared me, she said.

And you scared me, I said,

from the bathroom—already looking for makeup and cream.

October

The first cold morning, the little pumpkins lined up at the corner market, and

the girl walks along Hudson Street to school and doesn't look back.

The old sorrow blows in with the scent of wood smoke

as I walk up the five flights to our apartment and lean hard against

the broken dishwasher so it will run. Then it comes to me: Yes I'll die,

so will everyone, so *has* everyone. It's what we have in common.

And for a moment, the sorrow ceased, and I saw that it hadn't been sorrow

after all, but loneliness, and for a few moments, it was gone.

Delivery

The delivery man slowly climbs

the five steep flights of stairs

as I lean down to watch him walking up

as he's talking on the phone

and now he pauses

on the third-floor landing

to touch a little Christmas light

the girl had wrapped around the banister—

speaking to someone in a language

so melodic I ask him what—

when he hands the package up to me,

and he says Patois—from Jamaica—

smiling up at me from where he's standing

on the landing

a smile so radiant that

re-entering the apartment I'm

a young woman again, and

the sweetness of the men I've loved walks in,

through the closed door

one of them right now,

kicking the snow off his boots,

turning to take my face in his cold hands,

kissing me now with his cold mouth.

everything moving underneath

half alive   half awake

What tunnels through the loam?

What rises from the sheath of leaves?

Magdalene at the Grave

That long-gone year, that late summer afternoon

driving toward the cemetery

and when the rain started falling hard—and then harder

turning back toward home

and then—as if something were pulling me—

pulling into a driveway and back again toward the grave.

Ridiculous as it was to park and kneel where he'd been buried

—to kneel in the rain—I laughed out loud!

After a few minutes, I looked up and saw the other car idling,

the driver's window rolled down.

The tears I wept then were not tears of grief.

How many times must it happen before I believe?

What the Silence Says

I know that you think you already know but—

Wait

Longer than that.

even longer than that.

Magdalene at the Theopoetics Conference

Yes, the scholar said, but why ask your students

to write these close observations?

What use is it to notice the rusted drainpipe?

The young woman asleep in the library

her head resting on her folded arms?

Why should they look inside the petals of the purple tulip

to the yellow pollen-coated stamen?

Or under their beds to where the dust has collected?

One Day

One day the patterned carpet, the folding chairs,

the woman in the blue suit by the door examining her split ends,

all of it will go on without me. I'll have disappeared,

as easily as a coin under lake water, and few to notice the difference

—a coin dropping into the darkening—

and West 4th Street, the sesame noodles that taste like too much peanut butter

lowered into the small white paper carton—all of it will go on and on—

and the I that caused me so much trouble? Nowhere

or grit thrown into the garden

or into the sticky bodies of several worms,

or just gone, stopped—like the Middle Ages,

like the coin Whitman carried in his pocket all the way to that basement

bar on Broadway that isn't there anymore.

Oh to be in Whitman's pocket, on a cold winter day,

to feel his large warm hand slide in and out, and in again.

To be taken hold of by Walt Whitman! To be exchanged!

To be spent for something somebody wanted and drank and found delicious.

if this line is the beginning I might be—

If there is no beginning   ok then

no end

I would be grass?

The I the I   the me me me   What use

has it been?   Somebody loved me

Somebody left   Bones   Ash

Whatever flooded into the world   when

He   died   that   then

the moonlit path over the un-walkable water